THREAT

THREAT

Julia Webb

Nine
Arches
Press

Threat
Julia Webb

ISBN: 978-1911027621
eISBN: 978-1911027805

Cover artwork: © Natty Peterkin
Artist website: https://nattypeterkin.tumblr.com

First published May 2019 by:

Nine Arches Press
Unit 14, Sir Frank Whittle Business Centre,
Great Central Way, Rugby.
CV21 3XH
United Kingdom

www.ninearchespress.com

Nine Arches Press is supported through public funding by Arts Council England.

Supported using public funding by
ARTS COUNCIL ENGLAND

Contents

Family and Other Distractions

Evidence of Body

Body of Evidence

'The river coursing through us is dirty and deep.'
– C.D. Wright

spilling

(1)

the body does not consider your feelings
the body demands this and that
demands, commands, demands

(2)

body – unbroken wall of light
body – oh sun and rain – gloriousness of weather on skin
body – blame and guilt in equal measure
the body shrinking into itself in shame
body – solid stuff and liquid
the liquidity of the mind
that bedding down, that settling in
body – entrenched and entombed
body suddenly let go again, floating balloonlike above itself
body – holding it up, holding it off, holding it in

(3)

yes – you are a delicate flower
yes – you are a tree standing solid, pushing your shoulders against
     the wind
yes – you are drinking the world and everything in it – little sips
yes – tiny things upset the applecart of your mind
yes – pygmy pears and love apples
yes – peeling it off layer by layer
yes – slathering it on, burying something, that need for hide and cover
     and lost
yes – afraid to be really seen
yes – happiness in there somewhere, peeking out from time to time
yes – wall heart, cloth heart, balloon heart on its piece of string

yes – give it away too easily or don't give it away at all
yes – boulder where the heart should be
yes body, yes body, yes, yes, yes, body, body, body
yes body and its inconvenient lusts and longings
yes – open legs where the heart should be
deadly nightshade, piss flowers
yes – swamp sex stink of the hothouse, film of damp on the top lip
yes – pebble flowers, cactus spines
yes – the hive of you – your clicks and hums and buzzes
something falling out of you, something running, something flying
yes – the inner frenzy, the calm exterior
yes – you are the whole kingdom of body

Dates

'you can scratch all over but that won't stop you itching'
Depeche Mode – 'Dream On'

(the translator)

Step outside of yourself he said, and I did,
high-stepping from myself like a stripper,
pulling off my skin, trying to ease off my bones,
but the pit of me is wrinkled and dry
as a raisin at the back of the kitchen cupboard.
I drank the wine and sipped glasses of water,
waited inside while he slipped out to smoke,
answered his questions,
even when he forgot to wait for the answers,
smiled until I was a honey smear waiting for ants.
In the brisk cold of the walk home
I shook off the smell of his fags from my coat,
the brush of his beard from my cheeks,
there was a yearning in me it's true,
but I was waiting for something,
and heart said *NO*.

(the reviewer)

It didn't turn me nutsy,
it didn't soothe the crease or up the happy,
I waited and longed for gentle soft,
nothing was relax
and the energy bullish,
we were halfway up the hill of good
struggling to reach the top,
all over was grey
and the well was dry,
a leafbare forest in February –
nothing to hold or remember,
just another bone-bleached day.

(the old friend)

as if nothing else existed –
at least for a moment
like the dress you coveted for years
that belonged to your sister
but when she finally let you wear it
you bulged in all the wrong places

(the ex)

he had already started talking
and his voice filled the car
like that house you thought you'd miss
but never once went back to
the foreign neighbourhoods of the past

(the city)

I licked the road delicate,
ran my fingers down its heavily trafficked spine,
the city groaned with expectation,
shifted with longing beneath its rivers,
I stroked my fingers over its high rises,
traced its spidery outlines with the hot palms of my hands.
I could feel the aching in its concrete slabs and brick,
feel it arch its back towards the sky.
I was a gap the city longed to fill –
I knew that, and I acquiesced.

what I said was only the tip of the iceberg

the way as he looked into your eyes you closed them
the slap of a hand on bare skin
butterfly breath
meantime
the time between shallow breaths
the gut twisting with expectation
flat dead air
the way the man in the café keeps checking his phone
dead time
the time between something and something
how those waiting moments hang
differently weighted
the shock of the day's first coffee on the tongue
body as vacuum
body as foot soldier
as hand grenade
all the clichés you can think of
the stomach flipping backwards
somersault mind
imprint of teeth on skin like crimping pastry
flypaper mind
steamroller mind
all your billion neurons jangled and flighty
body as room on fire
as quarry
body as dumping ground
the gifts that the tide washes up
plasticine heart
lego heart
mouse heart
monster
the way we zombie ourselves

nothing spoken
nothing understood
nothing written in stone
goodbye for now he said
goodbye for now

Dear Moths,

you have made my house a circus whose clowns
have reverted to their true characters
eating up the beauty and the light,
everything turned grime and sawdust.

*

Each morning when I wake I check myself
and find another hole – some just pinpricks,
but others wide enough for the sun to fall into
dragging behind it its train of clouds and birds.

*

I am fluttery around my edges,
when I open my mouth only grime and sawdust flies out.
Soon you will have to tame me with a whip and chair.

*

Hold a light up to me and you will see
that I am more hole than human –
like a string bag. Everything snags in me
or falls right through.

*

Sometimes in the evening when I'm watching TV,
or reading a book, you flicker past
catchable as a wisp of smoke,
and here I am in my giant clown feet
crashing clumsily about the room.

*

I am wondering when your circus is leaving town,
and will you clean up the mess you made?
There is talk of closed meetings and forced removals,
but I am worried you might leave gaps
that nothing else can fill.

Kettle

If I hadn't swallowed the kettle
maybe I wouldn't have boiled myself dry,
but I watched you every morning
dangling a re-used teabag over the mug
and something inside me broke.

My wire is trailing over the toaster again
with that melted plastic smell.
The kettle makes me clumsy,
when I bend to zip up my boots
water comes cascading out
and those tiny bits of limescale
like flecks of dandruff.

Every morning it's you in the kitchen
clanging cups, the scrape of teaspoons,
blobs of margarine on the counter,
your razor plugged into the kettle socket.
My gauge is so scaled up
there's no telling what my capacity is.

She was a biscuit barrel or barrel shaped at least

as he kept reminding her
the bucket he kicked splashed lemony water up the wall
her face a crumpled tissue on the floor
the dog was whining outside the locked back door
the TV was querulous and mundane
the shopping was waiting to be packed away
the kettle was whistling on the stove
a child was shuffling on their bottom down the stairs

She was a biscuit barrel though whether empty or full was unclear
he was a barrel full of vinegary homemade beer
his contents leaking out across the floor
a child had shuffled down the stairs and let the dog in
in the other room the TV blared
the shopping was defrosting in the pushchair's tray
the kettle was still whistling on the stove

She was a biscuit barrel mopping the kitchen floor
he was cursing the kettle and the dog
shouting through to turn the TV off or else
his mood was vinegary and cold
the shopping was scattered across the floor
the dog was whining in the hall
a child was crying in the downstairs loo
the house was quarrelsome and sly

Good Friday

was the day I chopped off my own head
and blundered around the kitchen,
no eyes to see myself with.

I touched heat and hollow,
put my head in a pot to boil –
to still my breath and hush my tongue,

and when I was tender and quiet,
I served my head up on a white china plate,
apple-mouthed and gristle-chinned,

heard your ecstatic gasp.

Fun is particular and unkind

look at the sticky mark it leaves
it is a letterbox of useless post

fun is only allowed between the hours of 7.30am and 11.30pm
and on production of the correct permit

that's fun there with the bald tail and squinty eye
streaking off down the road

running away with next door's rabbit in its jaws
you can hear their children screaming

We is in the bank

We is number three in the queue
and gulls scream over the city,
and the gulls shriek *dump, dump, dump,*
fish and chips and sometimes *pie.*

We is behind the woman in the fox fur
whose hair is a silver helmet,
whose voice is a snort
as she importants herself on her mobile phone
and every ring has its own finger.

We is in the bank
and Small is roll, rolling on the shiny floor
while the rest of the anoraked queue
pull ugly faces because secretly
they would like to slide and roll too.

We is in the bank
and the queue is moving so slowly
it doesn't move at all,
and Small is tugging my dress every ten seconds
with an *are we there yet? Are we there yet?*

We is in the bank
with the mouth machines all along the wall,
some that spit notes out and others that suck them in,
and Small wants to press the buttons
but *no, no, you must not look*
at what other people's fingers are doing.

We is in the bank
eyes to the front,
someone sneezes their Decembers out
into the shared air and we breathe them in,
we do the slow shoe shuffle
and eventually after we have wait, wait, waited –

we put our lips to the glass
and voice-hug the worried woman
who lives behind the window,
and she points and shrugs,
sends us back out into the city of gulls.

Weir

Bikes piled on yellow grass, and a slither
of steps hacked from the river bank –
with their neon coating of weed,
the creak and groan of the swings
and the glory of boys in baggy y-fronts,
balancing on the metal bar of the weir,
the whiteness of their thin bodies dazzling,
how arcs of water flew from them
as they abandoned themselves to the jump.

Colt

Look at him all lank and fulsome
in his shining coat,
his rude health an insult.
He is stinking up the yard
with his piles of shit,
eating your best border flowers,
his head in next-door's bush.
He is not afraid of the whip,
but tosses his head,
haughty as a wronged royal.
In winter he overnights in the shed,
slip-shod hoofs pick their way
amongst cheap garden tools,
wide lips tug delicately
at the guinea-pig's hay,
his tail swishes
like a town-girl's ponytail.
When you bring him water
sloshing in the silver washing-up bowl
he looks you right in the eye
with something between
gratitude and disdain.

Elegy

brother – exploding tank in the dark of childhood
brother – open your lungs and *really* breathe
brother – the shock of the doctor's tread on the night stairs
brother – the thrill of sitting in Father's chair
brother – no smiles after the age of five
brother – if only you could have believed in something different
brother – pop open another can
brother – two years between you and sister, six between you and me
brother – strip a gun in sixty seconds with the power of your mind
brother – the cave, the pit, the depths of space
brother – shoot them all down, every single fucking one of them
brother – rocket out into the universe
brother – remember the water tower? What was the view like from there?
brother – the damage the pills did wasn't what you expected
brother – balloon body, sniper mind
brother – blind luck, blind justice
brother – so sorry you found us closed for business
brother – scribbling in your notebook with an empty hand

In the first hospital

your body turned into a cushion,
it was the drugs you said
and the daily puddings,
as if sponge and custard
could fix those bothersome brains.

The man in the next bed
was crying for his mother
and there was a woman
who kept knocking her head
on the wall, *come in,* she said,
come in, the door's open.

I can't remember now if we drank
tea or if we brought you anything.
You asked me if it was true
that dad once threw me on my head.

You never spoke of who had done it
or how it happened.
Your boy is precious, you said,
keep him safe.

Oh Brother

How is it that you miss each morning,
the thrill of waking warm and toasty
in a pillowed and quilted bed,
the insistent bird song, the sun's keening,
that irksome pressure in the bladder
that finally drives you into the cold
and down the stairs?

*

Did the world always fit wrong,
like those days you pull a sock on and off
and on and off because the seam won't sit right.
Was your view a different colour?
Did the morning smell bad?
Did the birds jangle like off-key bells?
Did your mouth taste like rust instead of mint or lemons?
Did sirens blare when anything touched your skin?

*

You were precious cargo,
did no one tell you that?
Someone's darling.
All babies should be dandled
on the knee of love,
kept from the jaws of the wolf.
A mother should build a fence
to keep the forest out,
not invite it in to mind the kids.

*

Holed up in your room, your plastic soldiers
and military strategies might have been knives,
ninja stars and real guns:
service revolver, shotgun, AK47.
In another time and place you might have been the shooter
instead of the one shot down.

*

Oh Brother,
we are fragile, delicate, not invincible at all,
a bundle of sticks and nerves
with a computer on top processing –
why red and not yellow?
Why this thing and not that thing?
Why his hand on your back,
his taste in your mouth.

My grief is not allowed

My grief is pumpkin, salt and diamante –
something too flash to be real,
fake tears for the one who has dried up.

My grief wears me in a pouch
around its neck,
my grief could ward off evil.

My grief is ash on the tongue,
a spent match,
a dog-end picked from the gutter.

My grief, my grief,
sometimes I yearn to smoke,
sometimes I fruitlessly wish.

The language of home hurts my mouth

It spies on me at night, peering in through the letterbox.
Though I left years ago, it hasn't let me go;

when I was six it tied a bit of elastic to my ankle
so I would always bounce back again,

when I was ten it inked its name on the insides of my thighs,
enjoying slipping its hand between my legs.

This is how it is with us – me running, it pouncing.
Mostly it speaks in screeches, the rising voice of accusation.

My hometown doesn't have an s, an a,
or any other friendly letter. All its sounds are hard.

Weeks and months go by now where I barely say its name
but its language lives inside me,

spills out at odd moments as *fucks* and *cunts*,
a whole town teeming with swear words.

Beyond that the shush of pines;
shoulder to shoulder silence, shoulder to shoulder dark.

Girls' School

A Golden Shovel after Les Murray

We are cows. They herd us from
one room to another so that
they can teach us that crumbly dry
kind of learning, that toothless
knowledge that falls to nothing, sucking
us dry, not even rules to live by
or tips for how to get along in the
outside world, just number fog, geography of hot or chilly
places we can never take our budding breasts and mouths.

They keep us believing that
we are small and insignificant, gasp
at the size of our stupidity, clap their hands loudly
by our ears to move us along, put us in
detention for the slightest murmur, plunge their hands inside our minds and twist and pull, keep us in
ignorance of the things that really matter, and
never ever praise us, never
show us the greener pastures, but breathe
in our faces breath so contemptuous it almost knocks us out.

Lessons

(1)

Miss, are you stuck between the absences? Miss, can you hear the ticks of the bell Miss? The clock on the classroom wall ringing? Miss, can you empty the day of stickmen and alphabet? Miss, can you slow speech of numbers? Miss, maths is so science Miss. Miss, are you registering this Miss? Blink your classrooms Miss. Open your algebra and sing.

(2)

Orange mustache Sir. Grass stains on the cricket slacks Sir. The race is on Sir. The race is three-legged Sir. Can you egg and spoon it Sir? I didn't mean to high-jump Sir. Sir, do you exist in the realm of the classroom or are you fully-fielded? Sir, your hair needs a trim – it's brushing your stumps, it deserves detention Sir. Sir, are you pure soccer?

Bus Station Toilets

after Jen Hadfield

(1)

Meet me at Hide Out, Hideyhole, Hidden,
our own little kingdom.

(2)

Meet me with a marker pen, half a pack of Players,
roll-on cherry lip gloss in a flowery glass bottle.

(3)

Meet me in the cubicle with his initials inside an arrowed heart.
We'll ask the walls about Mary and why she is a whore.

(4)

Meet me at our secret place, behind the bus station,
opposite the court house door for boys on probation.

(5)

Meet me at Damp-Cement, Izal, Jeyes Fluid,
Meet me by the cracked sink and the broken soap dispenser.

(6)

Meet me at Tears-Fall, Rain-shelter, Conference-Room.
Meet me there as soon as you can and tell no one where you're going.

Tell Me More Lies About Love

'What Will Change Me and When Do You Become'
– Laura McKee

because my home town has a hand between its legs

we spend too much time in public toilets –
smoking, scratching boy's names onto cubicle doors.

Imagine the shock of touching a pickled egg
buried inside his hot wrapper of chips.

No myths here, only rumours, streets you can't walk down
because you have been warned off, boys it's best not to look at.

Spaces find you: the concrete slope under the road bridge,
the shadowy space beneath the walkways at the bottom of the flats.

You'd rather lie through your teeth than confess your sins –
you might get a good hiding or your friend would stop being your friend.

There's a spyhole in the wall of your best friend's bedroom
through which her brother watches her get undressed.

Shake off the boy on the pushbike at the edge of the estate.
Make sure your Mum's friend never gives you a ride home alone.

The Moth

he says *you are a looker like your mum*
and he says *wowee look at the pins on that*
you are ripening like an autumn fruit
and he says *when you are 16 I will take you to the woods*
I can't resist
and *my wife's not interested in sex since the second child was born*
and he says *it's not fair young girls are so good looking nowadays*
and he says *you'll be a heartbreaker one day*
the boys will come flocking like moths to a flame

Grammar School Boys

They bundle in the doorway of the mobile classroom,
fall on top of one another,
flicking each others' heads.

They put snow down your bra
and spy at the toilet window
until you blow smoke in their eyes.

They crawl on the floor
and look up skirts with torches,
one of them touches the Latin teacher's breast.

They hoot and holler,
make legends of each other,
tell stories of what they have (and haven't) done.

They show you their penises
at every opportunity,
ask you to touch them.

The one you've loved secretly for years
says he'll come and visit you every week
if you let him put it in.

Horses

There were rooms with horses in them.
They were gathering in corners,
snorting by the fireplace,
dirtying the floor with their muddy hooves.

I imagined carpets of grass
troughs of oats and buckets of water.
I imagined sugar cubes
and crunchy apples on outstretched palms.

I had read too many
horsey stories as a girl.
These were no ponies: big
with sleek manes and swishy tails,

heads that reached top of the door frame.
They were slick and heavy
with wide nostrils and squarish teeth.
Terrifying and glorious,

they broke things without meaning to
and were unashamed to shit on the carpets.
They filled the house with their stink.

Gold Rabbit is teaching me how to smoke

he tells me to hold the cigarette between my fingers just so.
You are lucky to have a rabbit like me, he says,
his paw on my knee. *I am such a gentleman.*
I love Gold Rabbit but his constant crunching
gets on my nerves, his lust for green,
the way he sees things that aren't there.
I draw the hot smoke across my tongue
and down deep into my lungs,
it scorches my throat and I cough it out.
Gold Rabbit wags his carrot at me, his ears twitching,
it's not ladylike to suck so hard, he says,
you need to be more delicate.
Sometimes I wish it was Jade Rabbit I had brought home.

Public Bar, Central Hotel

Bill, who swivels on his stool to get a better look at your cleavage.

Bill, who tells you: *you are the type of girl men have affairs with.*

Bill, whose hand moves to his flies as he speaks.

Bill, whose leather car seats smell of suntan lotion.

Bill, who plays you like a drum, a flute.

Bill, who truth to tell – *what truth might that be?*

Bill, who by rights shouldn't.

Bill, his hand sneaking up your skirt.

Bill, who plans to retire with a caravan and a Jack Russell.

Bill, suburban, slacked and uncompromising.

Bill, shorter than you, but you pretend not to notice.

Bill, who promised you nothing but dry-heaves in a pub toilet.

Bill, too cheap even for a cheap hotel.

Bill, who silent-fucks you in the car park behind the bins.

Bill, who won't look you in the eye but buys you another vodka and orange.

Bill, twizzling his pinkie ring and thinking about his wife.

Bill, sheepskin jacket on, heading home.

Bill, *once*, you said, and that was the second time.

Just

He said her skin was soft, so soft, and young, he said.
He fed her smoked mackerel; she liked the smoky taste,
but oh the tiny pin-prick bones, so many of them,
so many, and the oiliness of his fingers.
And after lunch they climbed the green hill of the afternoon
with its attendant sun, he took her to the sawdust pub,
ales lined up, and the long drive back, switch off the headlights
and coast down the hill and she kept her scream balled up
at the back of her throat so as not to look stupid or too young.
And back, back in his house he night-slept on the sofa,
for *woman thing is such a turn off, such a turn off,*
woman blood and the dirty, dirty smell of her, he said
as he nodded off. *So dirty. Dirty, dirty girl.*
So she climbed the slippery stair into bed,
and woke later to his shadow-self looming up in the dark.
Is he looking for me, is he looking, is he coming to me,
no, no, turned away he is, what now, turned away,
he's at the cupboard, creak of door, thing in hand
and splatter-splat drops hissed and spat on wooden floor,
shake, shake, and he stumbled away, down again, down again.
Dirty cat, she whispered, *dirty old man dog.* But whispered
under breath lest the furniture-beasts that crouched around
in the black of his room come leering up to came fetch.

Denial

In I come all hangdog mouth and when your eyes
won't meet mine I slam behind the bar, rattle
the glasses out the drier and bang them on the shelf.
In your shortsleeve shirtsleeves, mucked up
to the elbows, you props up the bar proper,
mouth gobbing all sorts while they all fall about
laughing. Barry calls for another round and I see
from my eye-corner the way you toss back the frothy
dregs, hear your lips smacking against the glass –
those same soft lips that last night out back
pulled the nipple out of my dress and sucked it hard
making moans of the dark. The beer foams
into the glass all browns and lovely, and Barry
slides the coins across the bar with a leery wink,
and I know then you've told all. I hear their laughs
echo and the backslaps crack as you swagger
out back, cig in mouth before you're even out the door.

carport

my mouth is a carport with a broken light
I invite you to drive your tongue inside

but you prefer to hang around
in the street revving your engine

you are impatient for someone but not for me
my body is too big and broken

my head holds a world-sized headache
I use migraine as a pet name

my mouth is a carport with a broken light
there is a chest freezer by the back door

it is full of something dead

Sleight of Hand

Blink, you said, *and you will miss it,*
it's not like I hadn't heard that cliché before.
I opened the doors to you and you galloped in,
trampling the soft furnishings,
biting chunks of plaster from the walls.
I mistook your enthusiastic stampede for love.
Now you see it, now you don't.
was your other favourite saying,
though I didn't take it personally at first.
I missed the signs: your sleights of hand,
your disappearing rabbits.
It was only when you disappeared yourself
that I noticed the wizard's cloak
lining the inside of your hastily-discarded coat.

Consultation

Varying Hare munches your leisure,
puts you behind the longest fence in the world.
A spirit animal, she says,
does not always look like an animal,
act with impatience, repent with haste.
Varying Hare doesn't always make sense,
she likes to tell you her dreams,
is oblivious to your yawning.
It's impossible to follow her train of thought –
her mind hops from one thing to another,
runs so fast you can't catch up.
Varying Hare tells you that:
netting should be fixed to the line wire,
while she pours you a cup of tea.
She offers to bite your toes to cure
your broken heart – it's hare medicine.
That relationship was going in the wrong direction,
she says, *you're better off without him.*
Can a rabbit climb a fence? I don't think so.
She wipes the crumbs off the counter,
offers you another slice of cake.

A Hex on Love

after Rebecca Tamás

The hex on love is not really about the penis
or something hot and empty,
though love is about filling something up.
The hex on love is about tearing apart
all those smug photos and statuses
until they are coloured atoms spinning in space.
Love is mostly about validation,
if my fingers type these words and the world believes in me
then, perhaps, I can believe in myself.
The hex on love is not interested in padlocks
or hanging around on bridges.
The hex on love would make new rules about
when and where one can drink champagne,
it doesn't care about truffles or the asparagus
slowly rotting in the bottom of your fridge.
To hex love you need a fleecy blanket and a cricket ball in a sock.
To hex love you must shun internet porn,
wedding invites, spectacular sunsets.
To hex love change your relationship status to married
even though you are not –
they say it's better to look your enemy in the face.
To hex love throw away anything that reminds you of anyone.
To hex love you must first start believing in the solidity of the self.

Moon Party

you are too full to sleep
you are full of the moon
it is bursting out from inside you
it is shining its moon-face from your stomach
the moon thinks of itself as an emergency
it wants you to call 999 or 112 or 911
the moon never knows which country it is in
you are in a motel and the neon lights shine through the curtains
you want to birth the moon
but the moon is not going anywhere
it says it is fed up with hanging around in the sky
the stars get on its nerves with their incessant sparkles
the moon wants real fireworks
the moon wants a bonfire with tinfoil baked potatoes
the moon wants toffee apples and Halloween pumpkins
you go to the store with the moon and your credit card
the cashier asks when it's due and you say you don't know
she looks at the toffee apples and raises her eyebrows
she adds a free toothpaste sample to your order
they don't sell fireworks but they have birthday candles
you buy a moon-shaped cake and a box of matches
the moon and you have yourselves a motel party
you drink the entire contents of the mini-bar
and pass out on the bathroom floor

Family and Other Distractions

'Every group has its emperor.'
– Nuar Alsadir

Nothing could be done

'At six o'clock he'll be in / all antler and hill-breath.'
Em Strang – 'Her Indoors'

In later years he said they shouldn't have married
but she was the great persuader. The bones remember
their rows walking into town, roses twining
up garden walls, their voices rising oblivious,
three children, all of them mistakes,
in the big pushchair or trailing behind.

On later Saturdays he stayed home to redo
the housework. The hall smelt of floor polish
and Chelsea buns. The house was full to bursting:
the dog chewed her basket until all that was left
was a twig, cats crowded the tops of the kitchen
cupboards, ants swarmed through the window
and under the door, damp shirts were strung on lines
across a steamy kitchen, the living room was thick
with cigarette smoke, the 6 o'clock News blaring,
always somewhere a door slamming.

Brewing

In the dark Aggy Scragbag hears Ma and Pa
splitting the night open with saw-tooth words,
and up creaks the stink of something brewing,
something she sees when she sneaks downstairs

bubbling in its giant plastic bucket,
waiting to go into the barrel with the leaky tap.
When he sees her in the doorway Pa does an angry dance.

Aggy hot-foots it up the stairs and bangs
her bedroom door, lays between jaffa-orange walls
and prays for the star-people (the ones that crocheted
the sky) to come to her window and take her back,

but though she pokes her head up beneath the net curtain
the flat roof outside stays resolutely empty.

They told us we were made of Webbs and Humphries

Was that my Humphries hanging on the line in the kitchen
alongside the socks and the scratchy terry nappies?
Was that my Webb nestled in the pink plastic laundry basket
between the dirty knickers and Dad's lilac shirt?
Was that my Humphries the dog was chewing?
In the nighttime when we were meant to be sleeping
but were listening to the radio under the covers,
the Webbs and Humphries raged round our room,
arguing about who was better than who,
swinging from the end of the bunk beds,
jumping up and down on Brother's chest while he slept,
making him choke and wheeze.
By morning the Webbs had hidden themselves away
inside the built-in wardrobe,
and the Humphries had fled to the landing
where they played chicken in the flame of the paraffin heater.
Sometimes the Webbs and Humphries followed us to school,
treading on the backs of our shoes,
poking us, pulling our hair, calling us names.

Saturday was crumpet day

There was more evidence
in the bottom tray of the big pushchair
than I care to mention,
we were all hung about with shopping.
Fish paste on melted butter, yum yum,
sister said, her face a kipper.
Enough of that, snapped dad
marching into the kitchen.
Mum fluttered her shopping-bag dress,
her money-sore fingers.
Crumpets are round, sure enough, said brother,
but they don't make good ammunition.
Nobody laughed, we didn't know how to.
We settled down to tea drinking,
which is a serious business.

The Doll

was in our father's arms,
he butchered her daily,
first cutting off her head and arms
then her legs and feet.

He waved at us with her hands
from the kitchen window
as we bounced tennis balls onto the flat roof,
any excuse to climb on the fence.

By tea-time she was sewn back together,
her stitches clumsy, her head on wrong.
She crashed around the kitchen,
dropping hot fat onto delicate skin.

I'm all fingers and thumbs today,
she would say.

Saturday afternoons he nods off

in front of the boxing,
the fug of smoke around his head,
even the cats shooed from the room.

Not a thought in his head but the blissful quiet,
nicotine brain, the roar of the crowd,
a brown ale to warm the cockles,
not an aggravation of a child in sight.

Meantime we creep around the house,
barefooted thieves,
trying hard not to make a noise.
Mother's at the bottom of the stairs,
glaring, finger to her lips,

or in the kitchen kneading onion
into bright pink worms of mince,
the orange slime of egg yolk,
the lit'luns begging a treat.

Me – book open on the table reading,
someone, somewhere, in a headlock,
someone's lights punched out.

Radio Nights

I slide down deep beneath the covers

output may be subject to further
interruptions on the subject of snow

turn dials by torchlight
prop the heavy radio

knobs for eyes,
large square battery for heart

on bent knees
the nylon sheet crackles with static

imagine Luxembourg as a party shape
at the far side of the car park

the blue vinyl of the radio
like a cheese grater

music shreds itself into slivers,
drops down between the pillow and the wall

sentences left hanging

Aggy Scragbag reaches an age

and all hell breaks loose
tongues are unleashed from their moorings
like boats in a storm thrashing the shore.
It is thunder, snow, hail,
and blistering sun all at once.
In the street, cars stop suddenly,
boys on bikes follow her home talking inanely,
or even worse not talking at all.
Even the Smiths from opposite notice –
the oldest mimes feeling titties
whenever she walks past, the younger two
alright her now as if they hadn't ignored her before.
Ma and Pa's friends are worst,
she learns to keep her distance, stay by the door.

Owlet

(1)

My owl mother takes us shopping,
we try on nests and feather boas.
What about this? she asks
dangling a mouse in front of my face.

(2)

My owl mother asks us what we want for dinner,
we ask for sweet and sour ribs.
She undoes a jar of sticky sauce and smiles,
open up your chests, she says.

(3)

My owl mother is taking up singing,
her screech can be heard all over the house.
My sister wears earplugs, but I sit on the stairs
and empty myself of everything but her voice.

(4)

My owl mother leaves us with her owl father
and returns to find him trying to peck out our eyes.
I didn't think he'd do it to you, she hoots.
It's the first time that I notice her scars.

(5)

My owl mother has pushed me
out of the nest too early.
I sit on the ground squawking,
too late, she hoots, *once you're out you're out.*

Mother as Nuisance Phone Call

It has come to this
the reluctance to pick up
the holding of the phone away from the ear
no audience necessary
no one living up to
no one performing as they
nothing fair or kind
words piling across distances
drifting against the doors and windows of us
all the little guilts and blames
that pick at our scabs
that eat away at me
until I am covered
in a dress of cobwebs
and lightly finger-printed dust.

She is an unbaked loaf

proving in the yeastiness of her room

hoist your hellos from the ceiling to expose their most private parts

MAY ANGELS WATCH OVER YOU

She is a painting – thick slashes of acrylic
her brush strokes stored in carrier bags at the bottom of the bed

hand-knitted carers at 8am, 1pm, quarter to 5

I CAN'T FIND MY PENSION CREDIT LETTER

She is half-melted chocolate bars
Kit-Kat Mars Bar Fry's Peppermint Cream

legs like zeppelins have crocheted themselves minds of their own

NOBODY LISTENS

She is wind-chimes in the doorway
a sachet of instant cappuccino

Jiggle Dance Bird-Box Aspidistra

I KNOW IT'S HERE SOMEWHERE

She is a peace-pipe hung above the fireplace
all her hurts jiffling about the place

NO ONE DOES IT RIGHT

The days lap dangerously at the bed legs

She is the bird in the bird-box and at the window
the microwave's ping

no sister no

sister she ring me when i say
i tell her Mama is used up gone
and she say oh crap oh deary my word
but she also say she not come
and i use up the train to travel tracks
and track over the airwaves mobile
and she still insistent not come
and all the friends of mum blame
and isn't it no happy time already
blame blame suck them tears back in
and sister no want and no one want
but someone have to   bad bad business
friends flicker flicker in the hospital rest
and we undertake to outside woods
with carry on heavy and ice melt feet
and sing sing earth hole rain shiver
friends them no sister no in the wooden
hall guitar nephew and music music
eat eat art and full food trestles
then blam blam back in the van filled
for motorway long excavate home
and the real wide end of something
and still at the end no sister no

Resurrect

What if I could have upped you and walked you out of there
on your broke down legs, no haulage required,
just zipping across the space that lies,
and a big zing of push that pulled you – bish – out of that bed,
your feet as new as the dance within them?
What if we could have anewed, renewed,
fixed back in place what once was,
unbroken what was broke, be what some call healed?
Then you might be alive and in your smiles,
wearing the day light and airy as a thin summer dress
through which the wind runs fingers across your skin,
you might be up and away instead of down deep gone,
and I would be light as fluff through lack of guilt,
and we could, and we could, and wouldn't that be something?

Your mother is landlady of the dead house

She slides a drink to you along the bar –
where did she learn such tricks?
She used to be an ordinary woman,
with her peasant dresses and handicrafts,
she is even handier now, the landlord says.
Your mother pushes her breasts up and together
as if she has just discovered them.
Now she is out of her dress-tents she feels invincible.
You want to make her one of those warning signs
like the ones they have at the swimming pool
to help steer her through the choppy waters of lust:
no heavy petting, no bombing.
Your mother is pulling a pint,
the muscles in her arm bulge,
she leans across the counter
and whispers in a customer's ear,
her voice is breathy, girlish.
You want to sweep her into your arms
but instead you knock back your drink
and call for another shot –
tequila with its line of salt.
Oh mother you are a public bar
and I am the scratches on the counter
you tried so hard to remove.

Friday Night, King's Head

Some girl is pulling another girl's hair, and some other girls are in the loo skinning up, and Andy is trying to force his way into the Ladies with his watery eyes and wet lips, and it's your job to keep him out and keep his tongue out of your mouth, and the Heavy Rock Disco is playing *Paranoid*, and before that it was thumbs in belt loops for Status Quo, and Billy is shaking his blonde head like someone demented, ten years from now he'll be in the army cleaning his gun, his hair shorn off, and there's a row going on outside, a Cortina revving its engine, and someone's laughing, it sounds like a tree full of monkeys, but when you go outside it's the usual crowd sitting on the wall round the tree smoking, someone astride a motorbike, someone being sick, someone with beer thrown over them, a couple are kissing under the coach arch, the night screams and booms in your ears and though your eyes seek out the dark corners you can tell that Dan's not here, but here comes Andy dogging your footsteps, so you'd better keep moving, and if it was fifteen years from now he might be spiking your drink, someone buys you a vodka and orange, someone whispers in your ear, someone passes you a joint, back inside the bar the air is hot and thick with smoke, the music is pounding, you push through a wall of sweaty bodies, the D.J. you used to date plays your favourite Steve Hillage, the one you ask for every week, in twenty years you won't remember its title though you will remember the keyboard thrill, Roly is on the floor gyrating, his ageing mum in her leather jacket is leaning against the wall, two guys are shouting at each other by the speakers, a boy with a Mohican and acne passes something to a girl with dead eyes, you check the poolroom but Dan's not here yet, you dance to Fleetwood Mac, someone moves close, you feel his breath on your neck.

Brandon Road

the only petrol station in town
opposite the house with conkers
two pumps and a grumpy attendant
who always wears the same stained jacket
who offers you pink paraffin in a sealed can
because at your house no upstairs heating
the haunted ruin is right there next to it
no one dares to knock it down
release the ghosts
the petrol station turns its sulky back
they are building a new estate behind
grass turned up and over everyone knows it will flood
water meadow
the girl from your year with the freckles lives there
her dad's a chauffeur with a uniform and cap
the boy from the conker house becomes your friend
his living room is the size of a netball court
and houses a baby grand
his house owns a swimming pool and a poltergeist
it also owns his grandmother
who has walked here from some more glamorous era
hand me a cigarette would you darling
no one knows who haunts the haunted house
run with your fingers crossed as you pass its gate

street

we are a nation of rolling bins and cats in various colours
flame days are Mondays only and entail much blocking off
rain glues itself to the roofs shouting *what is this shiny wet*
pavement craves burst of hot so it can burn itself up
night moons up over the rooftops singing in owl voices
slowly brightens itself with baubles and tinsel
cloud fogs the horizon orange streetlight candles only
here come the small engines eating up the street
walk your bird here you are welcome but don't let it off the lead
and be sure to bag up its difficult children
this is a smeary neighbourhood at the best of times
hearts smash into one another beneath quilts and blankets
phones shout themselves sick with worry
something is night barking at the apex of the garden
pack up your fox tails missus   best to leave quietly

Evidence of Body

'The light has bored out of the body's long house.'
– C.D. Wright

you are on fire

you have accidentally swallowed the sun
you are shining like a midsummer picnic
you are setting and rising at the same time
you talk in solar flares
you want the sun to come out but it stays hidden
you are burning up
you could drink an ocean salt and all
you settle for a double vodka
the sun approves
it sends you to the bar for the bottle
the barman admires your glow
offers you peanuts a bowl of olives
the sun soon tires of his basking
you grab the vodka and head for the pool
the sun is scared of water   it never learned to swim
you choose a sun lounger
two cheerful tourists claim the beds next to you
you burn them up with your smile

Collapsing is a lot like anything else when you think about it

Collapsing is like standing up in reverse. Reverse collapsing is not a negative – think feet on floor, bottom on chair, the back firm and straight. Collapsing is less of a crumple and more of a slither, like a drunk slumping slowly down a wall. A wall collapsing is more than a simple kitchen-sink drama – think subsidence, think demolition, whatever you do don't think bomb. Bomb is like the collapsing elephant in the room, the thing we think about but don't mention, like ageing – you hope it will never happen. Unlike ageing the probability is somewhat slimmer. Collapsing is a slimmer version of bomb, the thing that we secretly dread. Dread lurks on every street corner, but we try to keep it at bay. Some of us keep it at bay by watching the news. The news allows us to feel like we are in control. We are not in control. We are not in control of our own collapsing. Some might say that we are not in control of anything; that it all comes down to luck or God. God is a collapsing concept that so far hasn't got us anywhere except into trouble.

12 Short Essays On Lens Replacement Surgery

the eye and the I are one / until they are not

tearing is not the same as tearing / you could lose all or part of something /
you are likely to feel unbalanced

tip right back / dazzle dazzle disco / lower the light / place towel /
small mercies

lines misremembered / your voice comes from far away / underwater

a sun / a star / the big bang / the kitchen bulb naked in its socket

you are a ploughed field with a headdress of gulls

an incision / an excision / when the lens is lifted / broken / you become
the swinging 60s

there is a happening above you / purple and orange blobs

towards in focus / between colours / a range of distances

not the shouting eye / not the all seeing / not the see no evil / not the day
cracked open like an egg / not the egg itself / not gelatinous gloop –
the vitreous body / not the aqueous humour / the crystalline lens

a descending curtain / an overcast sky / a sudden deterioration /
a fenland river steeped in mist

someone said breathe / you can't remember who or when

Lightening Up

She untitled her hair, her skin,
tried on the bath then slipped it off again
slick off a seal.
She untied her mind and let it float away,
it hovered above her for a moment –
a balloon set free but reluctant to leave the child's hand.
She untied the weight of words
and watched them flutter away
a slight flicker then gone.
She untied her better self and her worst self,
her *lady of struggle and articulation,*
she untied her weighty limbs, her solid trunk,
her awkward digits, her inconvenient sex.
She unmoored herself and threw away the paddle,
drifted haphazardly from the shore.
Lastly she hoofed out her fickle organs,
tossed them carelessly overboard.

expansion of

the body harbours stuff / the pain centre feels expansive /
and unending / spinning out and out / like it will never
stop expanding / other times the painiverse is imploding /
closed in on itself like a collapsing cake / pain assures you
that it harbours no malicious intent / it simply is / the body
has made itself into a shanty town / it gives refuge to pain
/ pain comes from far and wide / it queues up for food /
pain wants to phone out for more pain / to advertise that
this a good place to be / pretty soon the locals accuse pain
of all the petty crime in the area / later they will accuse it
of more serious offences / the body is unaware just how
much it can tolerate / pain shows it how miraculous it can
be / when pain disappears it is unclear whether it will be
coming back / and where it has gone / has it left of its own
volition / has it been imprisoned / is it waiting to be freed

Body as retreat from the world

body as a church on fire
body as belonging (and not belonging)
body as place-holder
body as betrayer
body as collateral
body as experiment
body as currency
body as threat
body as battering ram
body as punishment
body as political argument
body as evidence
body as statistic
body as cargo
body as bomb
body as peace sign
body as protest
body as occupation
body as housing estate
body as tower block
body as firework
body as parliament
body as terminator
body as terminal
body as garbage
body as shield
body as peace offering
body as refuge

It is naked late

and here we are
aeroplaning a flat space in the meadow
masking our body stink
with crushed grass
we could be grass angels
but no
the bruise of your lips
is anything but angelic
like the quick sting
when you press each spent match to my skin
I inhale the smoke of you
draw you into my lungs like a prayer
like a yoga breath
but we are nowhere near a meditation
our bodies zing and spit
the fizz of a grass stalk pulled slowly
across a nipple
a fistful of hair
the toothing of an earlobe
day lateness turning
as we swim here
on a tide of hay

Nostalgia

after Dawn Lundy Martin

dear one the sea smells of nostalgia
and I smell of nostalgia
and I smell of the sea
trussed up in nets of wanting you
your hand between my legs
a kind of clamping
when Alice and her mother were here
ripping down the ivy
I thought of you
all that dust
I imagined climbing up
my tubers needling their way
into your brickwork
you would rip me down
no doubt about that
or maybe use your shed poisons
dear one I taste nostalgia
I ache for your hardness
your salty smell

Love Poem to Loneliness

because inside is safer than outside
because of the human capacity to hurt
because every man for himself
because the cold seeps into your marrow
because the lid has fused to the box
because of the cushiony thrill
because no one is safer than someone
because they taught you not to walk on the grass
because the grass is always greener
because the wind in the leaves
because of all the things that have happened
because of all the things that might happen
because it's familiar
because you've told the same story for years
because you can't break the spell

All Shades of Empty

after Nuar Alsadir

No one told me that the train would go so fast,
have so few carriages,
that most of the seats would be reserved,
that there would be no refreshment trolley
until we were more than half way there,
that there might not be many stops
or that there would be so many,
that the view would often be obscured
by rain or sleet or fog,
that darkness would fall too early,
that we would be stuck outside
the station for hours,
that it would be too hot
or too cold – no happy medium,
that we would be surrounded
by people talking too loudly
or playing tinny headphone music
or spreading around their germs.
No one told me that the journey
would be so short, or so long.

Complicity

I am as complicit in my emergency exit
as you are complicit in my demise.

The way you rubbed your palms across my breasts
displayed a certain amount of disquiet,

negated somewhat by the casual way
that you lounged on the bed in your pants.

We are currently above London
but the bank of cloud is so dense

there's nothing to be seen.
I am as complicit in my arrival

as you are in my departure.
I have my photo ID and a home-printed ticket.

My passport photo depicts me as a child killer.
Someone once called me pussycat,

someone else called me pupski –
I obviously have some animal traits.

I am furiously writing my way out of an emergency
and the sunlight is blinding.

Last week was a cornucopia of snow.
How well do we know each other anyway?

We have years old shared memories –
shoes don't match the laces.

The wind is easterly so there may be turbulence,
we barely know each other at all.

All the Women

'all the women, all the women
of Texas flock towards it'
Hilda Sheehan, 'The Box of Books 1'

all the women, all the women
are inside me now
shouting that this is a fine day for it
that they needn't have brought their brollies,
their rain faces, their fold-up kagoules

whose voice is loudest I couldn't tell you

I speak acorns and buttresses
I speak water lilies and doves
the day is a wedding
and shortly we will all climb with our brimming glasses
aboard a vintage double decker

but the women, the women
they are building their bakeries inside me
they are making baklava and baking exquisite cakes
they are replacing my blood with confectioner's custard
and icing the insides of my breasts

and they are right *it is a fine day for it*
the sky is smiling widely showing its teeth of birds
no bombs are falling
we have 24-hour supermarkets and online shopping

and there are books, books galore on eBay and in libraries
we can pick them up and check them out
we can put them under our jumpers and take them home

but the women, the women
are camped on the edge of the deep dark pool
they are writing their epic poems on the inside of my skin
they are filling me up with shopping lists
chapters of novels, letters and bills
I am word confetti

I open my book beak and inadvertently sing

Notes

Bus Station Toilets was inspired by the shape and sound of the marvelous 'Nigh-no-place' by Jen Hadfield (from *Nigh-no-place*, Bloodaxe, 2008)

A Hex on Love was inspired by 'Penis Hex' by Rebecca Tamas (from *Savage*, Clinic, 2017)

Girls' School is a Golden Shovel – the end words of each line are taken from 'The Cows on Killing Day' by Les Murray (from *Subhuman Redneck Poems*, Carcanet, 1996)

Gold Rabbit is teaching me how to smoke – Han Dynasty poets called the rabbit on the Moon the *Jade Rabbit* or the *Gold Rabbit*. These phrases were often used instead of the word Moon.

Consultation – The varying hare (Lepus americanus) is also known as the snowshoe hare or snowshoe rabbit, a native of North America, the species is best known for the large size of its hind feet and for its fur which changes colour according to the season – brown in summer and white in winter. Line Wire is galvanised wire manufactured from mild steel and used for fencing mesh.

Nothing could be done – the epigraph is taken from 'Her Indoors' by Em Strang (from *Bird-Woman*, Shearsman, 2016).

12 Short Essays About Lens Replacement Surgey – some fragments in the poem are extracted from: leaflets/letters from the Norfolk and Norwich University Hospital and *Cataract Surgery* (NHS Choices).

All Shades of Empty – the title was taken from p3 of *Fourth Person Singular* by Nuar Alsadir, Liverpool University Press, 2017.

All the Women was inspired by a line from 'The Box of Books 1' by Hilda Sheehan.

Other quotes:

Quotes by C.D. Wright from the poems 'Everything Good Between Men and Women' and 'Provinces' (from *Steal Away: Selected and New Poems*, Copper Canyon Press, 2003). Quote by Laura Mckee from 'What Will Change Me and When Do You Become' (from *See You Soon*, University of Arkansas Press, 2016).

Acknowledgements

Thanks are due to the editors of all the print and online journals in which versions of these poems first appeared: *Algebra of Owls; The American Aesthetic; Ambit; Atrium; The Bohemyth; Butcher's Dog; Cake; Domestic Cherry; Fenland Reed; Ink, Sweat and Tears; The Interpreter's House; Lampeter Review; Meniscus; Molly Bloom; The Moth; Mslexia; Nutshells and Nuggets; Oxford Poetry; Poetry News; Prole; Proletarian Poetry; Smeuse; South Bank Poetry; Spontaneity; Under the Radar.*

"Good Friday" appeared in the Bloodaxe anthology *Hallelujah for 50ft Women* (2016). 'Carport' and 'Some Kind of Recovery' appeared in *Norwich,* ed. Sophie Essex (Dostoyevsky Wannabe Cities, 2018). '12 Short Essays About Lens Replacement Surgery' first appeared in *Christbel Hopesmith NHS Anthology* as '18 Short Essays About Lens Replacement Surgery' (November 2018). 'no sister no' was commended in the 2015 Stanza Poetry Competition and 'Just' was commended in The York Mix Competition, 2018. 'We is in the bank' won the Battered Moons Poetry Competition, 2018.

Thanks first and foremost to the brilliant Jane Commane for her unceasing encouragement and insightful editorial input.

I would like to thank Arts council England for a Grant for the Arts and everyone who has given feedback on these poems: Tara Bergin, Bill Herbert and the Happy Brutes; Norwich stanza members past and present; Heidi Williamson; Richard Lambert; Hannah Linden; my Friday students; members of the Goat/52 Facebook groups. Extra special thanks to Heidi Williamson and Pascale Petit for their close reading, and to Peter Raynard for championing poetry that speaks of working class life. Huge thanks goes to Natty Peterkin for the cover art.